Retirement Money Guide

A Firm Foundation for Your Financial Future

Eugene W. Hill, Sr.

RETIREMENT MONEY GUIDE

Retirement Money Guide
A Firm Foundation for Your Financial Future

Eugene W. Hill, Sr.

Copyright © 2024 Watchdog Publishing, LLC
All rights reserved.

No part of this publication may be reproduced, stored in a retrieval system, or transmitted in any form or by any means, electronic, mechanical, photocopy, recording, or otherwise without prior written permission of the publisher.

Published in the United States of America By
Watchdog Publishing, LLC
Grand Rapids, Michigan.

This publication is designed to provide accurate and authoritative information in regard to the subject matter covered. It is offered with the understanding that the publisher is not engaged in rendering legal, accounting, or other professional services. If legal advice or other expert assistance is required, the services of a competent professional person should be sought.

Thank You

I would like to thank my wife, Deborah, for her unconditional love and encouragement (she is my C.E.O. – Chief Encouragement Officer). She has sacrificed so much to support my career and business endeavors. Her wisdom and high moral standards have made the most substantive impact on my life. I would not be who I am today without her kindness, guidance, and unbelievable patience!

I've also learned a tremendous amount about the power of love and courage from my sons, Eugene, Eldrick, and Alexander Quince. They helped me become more generous, patient, and thoughtful. Because of them I wanted to become a better person. They gave me purpose and a reason to stop the old habits that were holding me back from reaching my full potential. Ultimately, because of them and my seven grandchildren, I am driven to show up every day at my best. I want to be as much as an example for them as they are for me.

I can't say enough about my extended family and the support and love that they have shown me throughout my career. Their steadfast love has pushed me to move forward with new ideas and concepts. No matter the situation, I have the assurance that they have my back!

I also want to thank my spiritual leaders, Henry and Carol Fernandez, Pastors of The Faith Center Ministries in Sunrise, Florida. Bishop Fernandez has been a tremendous influence in my life. Because of his holistic teaching and guidance, I have gained confidence and inspiration to write this book.

EUGENE W. HILL, SR.

Table of Contents

My Path to the Present	7
Building and Leaving Legacies	9
My Two-Fold Mission	12
Resisting Commitment	13
Being a Good Steward	15
The Core Principles at D & G Financial Services	17
1 – Long-Term Care	19
2 – Managing Financial Data	21
3 – Legacy Planning	22
4 – Life Insurance	24
5 – Retirement Planning	26
6 – Social Security Planning	28
Strategy One: Making a Definitive Financial Plan for Every Life Stage	31
Four Steps to Success	32
My Personal Mission	34
Interconnected Parts of a Complete Financial Whole	37
Your Financial Plan Should Be As Unique As Your DNA	38
This is All I Ask	39
The Three Financial Modules	40
Creating A Financial Roadmap	42
Planning And Investing Are Connected	43
Relationships Matter	45
Insisting on Integrity	48

Strategy Two: Make Every Day a Saturday — 51

Strategy Three: The Principle of 70/30 — 55
- The First 10% — 56
- The Second 10% — 58
- The Third 10% — 59
- The Remaining 70% — 62
- Developing A Spending Plan — 67

Strategy Four: Maximizing Medicare and Social Security — 69
- Medicare — 69
- Social Security — 73

Strategy Five: The Secure Act 2.0 and Legacy Planning — 79
- Secure Act 2.0 — 79
- Legacy Planning and Long-Term Care — 82

Strategy Six: The Younger Generation — 85
- College Funding Plans — 87
- Student Loans — 90
- Wedding Plans — 91

The Next Steps — 93
- The Key to Prosperity Is Cash Flow — 93
- Coaches, Agents, and Advisors — 94
- Teachers and Nurses — 96
- Money Pays for It, But Good Health Buys It — 97

Concluding Thoughts — 99

EUGENE W. HILL, SR.

My Path to the Present

I spent my youth in the Norfolk and Chesapeake area of Virginia, and following high school, I served for two years in the United States Navy as an administrator of aircraft maintenance. Once I completed my service, I utilized my aircraft knowledge to start a commercial aircraft parts company that I operated for more than ten years. During those years, I analyzed aircraft maintenance, directed technology services, and managed aircraft supplies for several commercial airlines as well as their aircraft maintenance facilities. I also traveled extensively throughout the country, honing my leadership and administrative skills.

In 1992, I left the aircraft industry to pursue my interest in insurance and legacy planning. I began as a special agent and registered representative for Prudential in the South Florida area. In 1999, I took the step of starting my own business as an independent agent. **I called it D & G Financial Services because I believe in the Dominion of God and Glory to God** and everything I do is for the Glory of God.

As an independent agent, I have the flexibility to represent a number of companies. I believe this is best for my clients, because it gives me the opportunity to meet their needs without being captive to one company. For the last 30 years, I have cultivated my business practices and client processes, while constantly striving to improve my skillsets as I meet the mounting needs of my clientele.

"I Called It D & G Financial Services Because I Believe In The Dominion Of God..."

I am also honored to be a Life Underwriter Training Council Fellow (LUTCF) with the American College of Financial Services, where I also serve as a moderator. I partner with independent CPAs, CPA firms, and expert tax-reduction consultants to make sure my clients maximize their tax savings.

Through the decades, I have been supported and flanked by my wife, Deborah, a native Floridian and retired nursing director for the Department of Health in Broward County. I re-located to Florida in 1979 and have called it home ever since, where we raised three sons.

Building and Leaving Legacies
Speaking of our children, I look back and believe that perhaps the greatest retirement advice I have ever given to our sons was that they manage their *education*. I made sure they studied and brought in good grades, but I also told them, "You don't have to decide if you are going into college, you just need to choose the college you're going into." Education was always paramount. It helps to build your legacy.

Indeed, planning and building a legacy has been a central theme to my advice to everyone over the years. Plan for the future and be prepared for whatever might come. Think about the legacy you will leave no matter where you are in life.

Twenty-three years ago, just two days before Christmas, this philosophy was tested in a way I don't wish upon anyone. On that day, we experienced a tragedy that shook our family to the core. My oldest son, who was in his early 30s, passed away, leaving a wife and two children. Fortunately, and this may be the only thing that was fortunate about this event, my son had listened to me and made sure financial safeguards were in place. Because of this, his family was able to retain their previous lifestyle. And his two children, who are now 31 and 28, were able to benefit from that financial security.

This event was a wakeup call to me, as I'm sure it would be to anyone. But I also use it as an example when I discuss planning with my clients. The tragic and unexpected event underscores the need to have things in place to take care of your family in the event you are not here. And it also encourages individuals to plan and take ownership of their legacy while they are still alive. In my mind, I honor my son's life each time I help someone else plan for their own family.

Our second son, Eldrick, had a 4.3 grade point average and 26 scholarships offers when he graduated from high school. He chose to attended the Air Force Academy where he was a standout football player, and graduated with a degree in civil and environmental engineering. About nine years ago, Eldrick retired as an Air Force Major and decided he could make more of an impact in the lives of others by helping them to leave a legacy for their families. He saw what I was doing in my practice, and decided to make a career move and join the practice. He now manages our office in Colorado Springs. This was a win-win for us in that I now have a business succession plan in place, if or when I decide to retire. But as I like to tell people, **"I won't retire; I'm just going to re-fire."**

"I Won't Retire I'm Just Going to Re-fire."

Our third son, Alexander Quince, graduated from Florida State University and has over 30 years experience in the news industry. He has won three Emmy's and currently works as a regional news director for a major network Cable TV in upstate New York. He's also responsible for their news output in Rochester, Albany, Syracuse, and Buffalo. Even with these accomplishments, I am most proud of the fact that he is an ordained minister and servant of god.

I feel very fortunate that we had finances in place and our sons and their families have been able to land on their feet, regardless of what life dealt them. Our personal legacy has now grown to seven grandchildren, ranging in ages from 18 to 31, with several of them in college. Two attend historically black universities, Albany State University, and Florida A & M University. The youngest is now a freshman majoring in political science and the University of Georgia.

Knowing that you have built a legacy and financial security for your loved ones is a joy that is unparalleled. And the opportunity to share this joy with clients, helping them develop financial security and financial freedom while building a legacy for their family and loved ones, gives me the greatest job satisfaction possible. It's what motivates me to get up and go in the office day after day. Sorry, Eldrick. I'm not ready to bow out yet. I'm having too much fun.

My Two-Fold Mission
My two-fold mission is not only to educate my clients on the importance of financial planning, but also to create a lifelong personal relationship. I have found that the best way to do this is by listening. People tend to do business with people they know, like and trust, and it is my desire to develop those relationships with everyone I meet, without pre-judging.

I truly believe that everyone deserves to have a better future, and as a company, we strive to make sure the plans we structure for our clients protect them from market crashes, give them the upside of the market, and give them tax-free income during retirement.

I also firmly believe in an educational approach. I believe in innovative financial strategies, solutions and planning that result in financial clarity and overall financial health, and I want to make sure my clients have every opportunity to understand how all the pieces work together. I get excited about showing clients how they can reach their financial dreams by offering creative solutions through an open and transparent process that leads to financial independence.

Some of the things you may have heard before are: "People are going to fight you or they're going to flee from you." They are going to push back and say things like: "I don't need advice," "I don't need to worry about it," "I've got plenty of time to put a plan together," or "I'm too young." Yes. I've heard them all.

Resisting Commitment
What I know of these types is they resist making a financial commitment because they don't see the importance of doing it. Sometimes they cancel their appointments and reschedule. They seem more interested in immediate rewards than

planning for their financial future. But this attitude fades as they reach their 50s and 60s and are planning to retire in the next ten years.

"It's a Fear of Outliving Their Money"

During initial meetings, I like to ask this question: "What is your greatest fear?" And the answer is not a fear of illness, or growing old, or dying. Instead, **it's a fear of outliving their money**. This is the force that brings them into my office, time and time again. It's like a person who is sick or is being sued or is having financial difficulty. They need help and advice and want an appointment with a professional who will give them a solution or provide a prescription.

Because of this, I have learned to run our office practice like a physician, lawyer, or CPA. In every meeting, I prioritize listening. I then try to bring each client out of their comfort zone and inspire and empower them to create a plan for their financial future. And I address their fears by educating them. I take the time to detail how each financial vehicle impacts their long-term legacy, and I know clients appreciate that level of detail and education.

We prefer to see clients face to face, but during the Coronavirus epidemic, the opportunity to meet clients virtually became more mainstream. I am thankful that we were able to adapt to this changing business climate quickly, and because of the virtual service we added, we now work with clients in over 20 states.

Being a Good Steward

The other topic I enjoy discussing with clients is how we can all be good stewards of the finances that God has given us, which is based on Biblical principles. I have been honored to be an associate pastor of The Faith Center Ministries in Sunrise, Florida for nearly 30 years, where I am a recognized authority on financial planning, Biblical stewardship, organizational management, estate planning, retirement, Medicare, Social Security Maximization, and insurance planning. With that position, I have been given many opportunities to have faith-based conversations with people from every imaginable background. What they have in common, though, is being a good steward. And that's the core premise of financial planning and legacy building.

In conclusion, D&G Financial Services is built on prioritizing ongoing relationships with people by listening to and educating every client that walks through the door. We build legacies by implementing creative solutions and using a complement of experts, while following Biblical principles for being good financial stewards. If someone accused me of being a lifestyle guru rather than an empire builder, that would be OK. I wake up because it's my ministry and my business, and I get to work with people I know, like and trust. For that, I will be eternally thankful.

Eugene W. Hill, Sr.
DGFSINC.COM
954.747.4850

EUGENE W. HILL, SR.

The Core Principles at D & G Financial Services

At D & G Financial Services, our mission is to provide the families and businesses we serve with innovative financial planning, strategies, and solutions that result in financial clarity, security, and overall financial health. We do this by making strong personal commitments that lead to life-long relationships.

A mantra that I have used since I founded my company is: Integrity, Service, and Excellence. I insist on that with all our transactions and advice. Our insistence on integrity (and the reason it is priority #1 and priority #2) is not only about giving honest and fair advice, but also telling people what they need to hear and not just what they want to hear. And for us, excellence and service do not mean absolute perfection, but we do make every effort we can to serve your financial needs.

Our custom-tailored approach not only meets short-term and long-term needs, but it also helps our clients realize their financial dreams through creative solutions that utilize an open and transparent process. We empower each client to navigate today's complex financial world; and we customize a plan to fit their needs, their family's needs, as well as the needs of their small and large businesses.

We now have two offices, one in South Florida, and one in Colorado Springs, CO. As I mentioned above, I'm proud to say the Colorado office is operated by my son. As a multi-generational family business, we easily relate to the needs of other families over generations. We work across platforms and have a consultive business practice, and we work with a team and develop strategies best suited to meet the needs of our clients.

One thing we do right away is develop a financial roadmap that is tailored to a client's needs. Most have never gone through this process. When we do that, we find that many are caught off guard when they realize that their current "plan" may not allow them to outlive their money. We have also found that many new clients are weary, if not recovering from the money they lost because of market volatility.

We also make sure to expand their education on how to account for taxes during retirement, and which ways they can draw tax-free income upon retirement. For many clients, these conversations are enlightening, and perhaps even frightening. But once again, we emphasize the importance of sharing what people *need* to hear, not just what they *want* to hear. And then we build a retirement and legacy-building plan together.

Finally, we believe in an educational approach to financial solutions, and we develop a custom-tailored plan that puts each individual client on the road to financial independence – using tools and methods they come to understand. We do this through six separate categories of portfolio management and analysis, detailed below.

1 – Long-Term Care
As the baby boomer generation ages and the demand for care in their senior years increases, new methods of paying for that care have surfaced. In addition, individuals may look for assistance from life insurance and annuity policies that may include features that provide enhanced benefits if the policy owner becomes impaired (subject to certain requirements). Because of the many options that now exist, one of the greatest areas of education for our clients is what we refer to as long-term care.

Long-term care refers to medical and support services for those who have difficulty in executing routine daily functions, or those individuals with prolonged or degenerative illnesses, cognitive disorders, old age and/or other conditions. Nursing homes are probably what come to mind first when discussing long-term care, but long-term care can also include assisted-living facilities, continuing-care retirement communities and home healthcare, among others.

One reason long-term care planning warrants more consideration today than in the past several decades is because we're living longer lives. According to the U.S. Department of Health and Human Services, 70 percent of people turning age 65 can expect to use some form of long-term care during their lives. Not having a plan can mean that costs fall on younger family members, causing a financial strain, or on a retired spouse, leading him or her to deplete their own retirement savings.

Since dramatic changes in our health can surface quickly and without much warning, it is extremely beneficial to have a sound plan to fund long-term care, should it ever be needed at any point in your retirement. We consider this to be a critical category of portfolio management, and we know that preparing clients for a long and comfortable retirement gives *everyone* in the family peace.

2 – Managing Financial Data

It wasn't that long ago that managing your financial lives meant keeping track of dozens – if not hundreds – of documents like trusts, wills, powers of attorney, insurance policies, investments and more. They were squirreled away in drawers, boxes, grocery bags and in the best of scenarios, a safe. But thankfully, there is a product called Generational Vault – your virtual safety deposit box – that provides a far easier way to keep track of the many vital documents. Similar to how your doctor and medical team monitor your prescriptions, your appointments, and your various test results, our Generational Vault is your *one location* for all your financial needs.

Family members can rest easy, as well, knowing that they don't need to track down a dozen documents or remember computer or safe passwords to find what they need during an unforeseen emergency. One call. One location. We will keep everything organized and handy for you, so you and your family members can focus on what's more important during the critical times – each other.

3 – Legacy Planning

Proper legacy planning is another key element of a successful retirement strategy. With legacy planning, we help you ensure that your legacy includes caring for your loved ones even after you have passed. That also includes making sure your final wishes are respected.

"It is Important to Carefully Plan for the Transfer of Your Assets to Allow the Wealth that You've Worked Hard to Accumulate to Serve a Meaningful Purpose During and After Your Life."

We help you plan your legacy in a variety of ways based on your unique desires and whether it's most important to you to preserve assets for future use or transfer your wealth to beneficiaries.

It is important to carefully plan for the transfer of your assets to allow the wealth you've worked hard to accumulate to serve a meaningful purpose during and after your life. From starting the conversation with you, to guiding you through the actual transfer of assets, we educate you on the process and walk side-by-side with you through every step.

Creating a strategy for your legacy is more than simply managing estate taxes. We use a number of methods and tools to protect your wealth and ensure it is transferred as you desire – and in a way that has the least impact on the principle. We have a team that helps with:

Wills
- Revocable Living Trusts
- Powers of Attorney
- Advanced Medical Documents

In addition, we review term and cash-value life insurance, and we discuss long-term care insurance policy options. These policies are configurable in ways we have never seen before and can be designed to serve in numerous helpful capacities.

Overall, legacy planning and preservation of your wealth and assets require a coordinated effort. We feel satisfaction only when we have provided protection and peace of mind to you and your loved ones, and when we have defined the channels in which you wish to eventually distribute your wealth and assets you have worked hard to accumulate.

4 – Life Insurance

Although some people view life insurance as a replacement for lost income or a way to pay off debt after the passing of a loved one, it can also offer a number of benefits that make it a valuable tool to consider when planning retirement.

First and foremost, life insurance provides peace of mind and a degree of comfort for the policyholder (the insured) that their loved ones (the beneficiaries) are provided for financially in the event they pass away. In addition, life insurance can be a sensible solution for many small business owners to help protect the financial future of their business if something should happen to them.

Aside from those more commonly known benefits, life insurance can also help reduce or avoid certain taxes. Some of these benefits may include:

Death Benefits:

- Policy death benefits paid to beneficiaries can be set up to be income tax-free.
- Some life insurance policies can allow the

death benefit to be accelerated out before the insured's death due to terminal or chronic illness, and that benefit may be income-tax free.

Tax Advantage Exchanges:

- The insured may exchange their existing life insurance policy for a new life insurance policy, and the investment gains on the original contract may be tax free.
- The insured may exchange their existing life insurance policy for an annuity, and the investment gains on the original contract may be tax free.

Policy cash values:

- Cash values may grow tax-deferred during the insured's lifetime.
- Income from cash value, when properly structured, may not be subject to income taxes.

Because D & G Financial is an independent insurance firm, we shop dozens of insurance carriers to find rates and product solutions that fit your specific needs and goals. Unlike advisors tied to a single company – what I call "captive agents" – we are not relegated to a single line of products or brand name. As a further service, we are happy to offer complimentary reviews of your existing life insurance contracts. New and creative policies are being created all the time. I always encourage a review of the contract you have, just to make sure it is the most beneficial for you in the current landscape of offerings.

5 – Retirement Planning

At D & G Financial, we believe that choosing the right investment strategy is at least as important as the actual dollar amount you have saved. You've worked hard for years to save for retirement, and a wrong step now could eliminate years of hard work to build savings. And I hate to say it, but I've seen the aftermath of clients that took a wrong step before we were involved. It can literally change everything.

When we meet with you as a client, we review *every* aspect of a retirement plan with you to make sure you and your loved ones are best positioned to enjoy a happy and worry-free retirement. Does your existing plan consider recent changes to the law? What about the fact that taxes are at one of the lowest rates in history?

We go over these factors and consider every investment vehicle with our clients, so that we can together build the best retirement and legacy plan possible.

In each case, we look at a client's unique mix of assets, including everything from bank accounts, pensions, and Social Security benefits to estate plans, wills, taxes, insurance policies and more. Our services and strategic partnerships allow us to integrate all aspects of our clients' wealth into a coordinated effort. Our end goal is to create financial clarity for you and your loved ones, and to promote multi-generational wealth. Our services include:

- Insurance Planning
- Beneficiary Review
- Retirement Strategies
- Financial Needs Analysis
- Analysis of Present and Future Expenses
- Estate Preservation
- Income Planning

When you work with us, we organize your financial, estate, and tax-preparation materials into a single, customized proposal. We believe an all-inclusive plan is the most comprehensive and fail-safe retirement strategy, and it can only be done when all aspects are considered and all teams are coordinated. Instead of focusing on just a few specific products, as many financial services professionals do, our experience has proven that our clients' needs are best fulfilled focusing on processes, and most importantly, people.

Importantly, making a recommendation on a retirement strategy is never, ever a one-size-fits-all proposal. When you work with us, we provide you with a framework that aims to satisfy your retirement income budgeting needs, while also satisfying your risk tolerance and growth expectations. A retirement strategy isn't something you do once, but rather something that evolves, and that you revisit throughout your retirement. Knowing who to turn to for advice, and knowing that we welcome revisiting plans at any time, can make a world of difference.

6 – Social Security Planning

If you are like many retirees, your Social Security benefit represents decades of hard work and may be the foundation upon which you plan to build and grow your retirement income. Though most Americans have some basic familiarity and knowledge on the topic, few can determine — on their own — the right way to file so they are able to maximize their benefit and carefully integrate it into the rest of their retirement strategy.

At D & G Financial, we help our valued clients develop a clear understanding of their investment in Social Security, and both educate and inform them when they should start accepting their benefit. Delaying your benefit may potentially increase your benefit amount by as much as eight percent per year. And we discuss when and why that is the case.

There is a lot to know about Social Security, and it is important for you to be educated so that you head into retirement with a plan on exactly how you will rely on your benefits. Our firm is committed to helping you get the most you can out of your benefit, so you can take one step closer toward a comfortable and enjoyable retirement. **We also emphasize that there are no bad questions.** Social Security benefits are a complex matter, and we believe the best decisions are made only when you have a firm understanding of the options.

When you work with D & G Financial, we provide detailed explanations to questions like these:

- What is your Social Security benefit amount?
- When is the right time to start accepting your benefit?
- Are there different options if you are married?
- Does earning additional income while you are on Social Security impact the value of your benefit?
- Do you pay tax on your benefit?

Then, we collectively brainstorm how to best accomplish your legacy goals and maximize your benefits. The result is an approach to social security that not only provides the greatest benefit to you and your family, but also is understandable and executable. That's when we know we have met your needs.

Strategy One: Making a Definitive Financial Plan for Every Life Stage

As I said earlier, many individuals don't seek our advice until they begin to fear they will run out of money after they retire. And unfortunately, that sometimes means they wait until it is too late to put money aside for a healthy financial future.

"We Want to Be the Welcome Guest, and Not the Worrisome Pest."

To avoid this, we sit down as early as possible to make sure people are well-prepared for the future. We also tell people that we want to be the welcome guest and not the worrisome pest. We don't want to bug you, but we will need to do a strategy assessment that will document every detail of your financial picture and then create a definitive financial plan for every stage of your life. And what we create will be a plan that matches your needs, your potential, and your aspirations. Of course, as in everything else, we can only help those who want to be helped.

So, with this financial fear in mind, I want to emphasize the importance of this chapter. Whether you are single or married, whether you have children or not, whether you graduated college or not, and whether you are young or facing retirement, **you need to commit to planning your financial future**. I can say this until I have no voice, but without good planning and good guidance, your dreams of a comfortable and secure retirement can easily turn south. There are a thousand ways you can find yourself financially struggling, rather than financially secure.

Four Steps to Success

To put this in the best perspective, it is a simple four step understanding of what we appreciate most when we offer our professional services. We want our clients:

- To Be Likable
- To Be Coachable
- To Afford a Plan
- To Be Committed to a Plan

These may seem obvious to some, but to us they represent the ideals we hope every client exhibits when they come to us for advice. These are also the same expectations we place on ourselves. I tell people that *we don't chase, we work at your pace.* Our system is designed to work with people who are committed and motivated.

And I can share an example of how this works. I recently talked to a young man who's an electrical contractor. He's a business owner, and we established a revocable trust for his family. He called me because he was concerned that he didn't have anything in place. Here he was with a business that was successful, and a wife who had most of her affairs in order, but he needed to feel comfortable with his own finances. This was someone who was telling me he was motivated. He wanted to share his numbers and learn what I had to offer. We were able to implement a financial roadmap for his business and personal affairs.

In these cases, we share our preference to work with both the husband and wife whenever possible. It's not fair to both if one is missing from the table. Also, when they come together, it allows us to see both sides of the ledger – both sides of the same coin. Together they are united and better decisions are made.

To accommodate every person who walks through our doors, we provide multiple platforms for those who are pre-retirees (those in their 40s and 50s), for those who are about to retire (late 50s and early 60s), and for post-retirees who are 65 and over. We also work with people who are moving from one company to another, who are small business owners, and those who have concerns about their qualified accounts, IRA rollovers, and taxes.

Most importantly, at D & G Financial, we follow a mantra. It is something I follow personally, and it is an expectation I have for both our employees and our clients. It seems simple, but I believe it could define whether you fail or succeed. The mantra: ***develop a mission and a purpose and then find a ministry or a business to make that happen.***

"Develop a Mission and a Purpose and Then Find a Ministry or Business to Make That Happen."

My Personal Mission

My personal mission is to address and remove the poor relationship most people have with money. In some cases, this poor relationship leads to a poverty mentality and a multi-generational mindset shift – to the downside. This can be prompted or exacerbated by how someone was raised, or it may be a combination of other social, ethnic, and economic factors. But in many cases, the underlying issue is simple: people spend more than their income supports.

When I try to understand a complex situation such as what fuels a person's poor relationship with money, I tend to ask questions that may be startling. For example, I like to ask, "What three things do you want financially that you don't currently have?" "What's keeping you up at night?" "What motivated you to call me up to put a plan together?"

And as long as I'm not getting a strong adverse reaction, I don't stop there. "Why don't *you* think you have the things that you want?" "What three things do *you* want to discuss and accomplish or achieve?" "How do *you* feel about your financial situation in general?"

And regardless of what I discover that has framed this person's relationship with money, it is my mission and purpose to meet them where they are on their journey and help them find a platform and plan that will meet their needs. I want to be the hope *and the solution* they need and seek. This is why my ministry, and my business is about getting people to manage their money.

I also don't want clients to worry about their past, but instead learn a better way to compartmentalize their money. I want them to implement a 30-day plan, then a 90-day plan, and eventually graduate to an annual plan. I suggest early on that my clients use a receipt tracker or calendar to track every expenditure and write it down. **Because you can't expect what you don't inspect.**

***"You Can't Expect What
You Don't Inspect."***

I have found *overwhelmingly* that when people categorize every purchase they make and reconcile their bank and credit card accounts, they learn the dirty truth about where their money is going and how I can help them. Quite often, they are shocked. That's when I know I really have their attention.

Interconnected Parts of a Complete Financial Whole

This also summarizes my holistic approach to money. **All financial issues**, whether they are daily expenses, savings, investments, monthly budgets, long-term debts, or retirement dreams, are interconnected parts of a complete financial whole. I want each client to understand and use the complexities of our financial systems to their advantage, and I also want them to know all the rewards and nuances of hard work. But they will never get there if they don't first inspect their present spending.

I am pleased to report that most of the people I coach or call clients begin to reassess their relationship with money once they see that I truly care about their circumstances. They start to get their houses in order, and they come to me to proudly say they are putting away money each month. Mind you, it might be just $100 or $200 per month, but I can't tell you how critical it is that their mindset has shifted. They are watching their expenditures; and they are thinking about their future. I beam with pride when I hear things like this.

Many also follow my advice to find ways to increase their income. Some start side gigs. Some ask for a raise or start working more shifts.

And when we do an annual review, I have to tell you, I feel like I can barely contain my excitement. These clients have more confidence; they have a mission; they have a purpose. Their money, their ministry, and their business have new meaning. And they also can barely contain their excitement. They are achieving things they previously never thought possible, and the world is their oyster.

Like I said, Eldrick, I regret to admit I'm having too much fun to retire. I'm sure you understand. But on the upside, you should have some very happy clients to service if my re-firement ever directs me elsewhere…

Your Financial Plan Should Be as Unique as Your DNA

To create a perfectly definitive financial plan for every life stage, I believe that each client deserves a "DNA Approach." This is the opposite of the cookie-cutter approach used by many financial planners. I liken our DNA approach to being as unique as your DNA, meaning this approach is for you and only you. In fact, it is made in your image. I couldn't use the approach with someone else, because it just wouldn't suit them.

Our DNA Approach is intended to be so specialized that no two people, not even identical twins, should receive the same planning advice. For each person, the myriad of financial structures that come into play are very different. Their careers are different; their income potential is different; their spouses are different; their personal health is different; and most importantly, their retirement dreams and goals are different. A cookie-cutter approach ignores all of this and will never provide what a client needs or deserves.

This is All I Ask
What I ask of each client is that they give me their numbers – their income, their expenditures, their savings, their investments – and I will design a plan specific to them. I will use real numbers to show them what I anticipate will be their Return on Investments (ROIs), and I will go through every point at which they may be exposed to additional taxes or to the cycle of inflation and interest rate hikes. I call this hyper-personalized process "Retiring Up."

And when I ask for numbers, let me be clear: I want specific and detailed numbers, not approximations. I don't want underestimates of what they owe or overestimates of the appraisal on their properties. If the numbers aren't precise, the clients don't buy in. Rather, I want my clients to see their own DNA in the numbers, and to have 100% ownership in the plan, because that plan is 100% about them.

My experience tells me if you are not able to take ownership in a plan – to look at it and say "that's 100% me" – you are merely spinning your wheels. My time putting the plan together and your time reviewing it with me is wasted. We'd both be better off if I found another client who will give me real numbers, because they are far more likely to follow a plan I put together.

The other fact I have learned from experience is those who don't take ownership tend to blame others when they are not successful. That is why I emphasize to my clients that I am not the owner; I'm just an advisor and facilitator. You need to see yourself in that plan. If you can't, we won't go far.

The Three Financial Modules

Another approach I utilize is to ask each person to complete three financial modules that I give them. I expect them to complete the first module before going on to module two, and to finish module two before tackling module three. Module one includes basic information like your name, address, spouse, and extended family. Module two dives into income and retirement plans, and module three asks you to list all assets and liabilities. We call these modules our "Smart Fillable Platforms."

Here is the benefit of these modules: they not only educate clients on the various aspects of money management, but they also require participation and input. I'm essentially getting "skin in the game."

Additionally, I provide tutorials and videos that show which documents and statements will be needed when clients work with us. These include specific interest rates and certified appraisal numbers. I use this information to provide clients with the most accurate information possible, which leads to the best, and most informed decisions.

We also begin a strategy assessment early on, during which I ask a lot of questions. Admittedly, I tend to bring my personality and philosophy into these sessions. I like to approach each case like a doctor would evaluate each patient and do a thorough financial examination. I use this analogy because each financial problem I discover will need a prescription. And like any physician knows, you can't give a prescription without an examination. That would be malpractice, and likely fruitless.

Creating A Financial Roadmap

Most of the people I meet with have not done a complete financial evaluation. Many have never been given a financial roadmap to guide them. The strategy I offer is a prescription to alleviate their fears. It includes a platform of 11 questions that will analyze their risk propensity and their past relationship with money.

We use this information to build a complete strategy assessment. My team analyzes the client's numbers and answers, and we look for dispersions that are not congruent. Through this process, we can predict what a client's finances should look like in five to ten years and identify the deficiencies that will arise over that time. We use the composite data and provide graphics that can give the client a realistic picture of their future lifestyle.

"I Tell People That the Best Time to Fix Their Financial Problems is Right Now."

I tell people that the best time to fix their financial problems is right now. I ask people to choose who they will serve and to get their house in order, because the longer they wait, the more it costs. This is because with money, the decisions that benefit us the most are usually those we make first. Those who create a financial plan early in their life and use a disciplined financial approach throughout their lives will enjoy a more secure retirement later in life.

Planning And Investing Are Connected

Whether you have a home office, run a small business, or work outside your home, planning and investing are connected. Good financial plans always capitalize on how you can invest your money, and even your time, to benefit your later years. Good financial plans also track every expense and use an itemized approach to address all the pieces of the financial puzzle at the same time.

Because of COVID and the advances in virtual technology, more people are using their computer for business and communications. By doing this, they are keeping their overhead down and saving money that would have gone to food, travel, and possibly lodging. This savings can be redirected to an investment that could benefit a business or retirement or plan.

***"You Can't Solve a Problem if
You Don't Know You Have a Problem."***

I have heard it said many times that you can't solve a problem if you don't know you have a problem. This is certainly true if you don't have a plan in place to manage all your expenses and investments. And I have seen this play out many times over the years.

Tragically, this happens regardless of income, age, or money in the bank. People will always lose money in the market. Some will lose just a few percentage points; some will lose the vast majority of their investments. The real pain comes when they try to recoup the investment. A 30% loss in the market will require a 42.8% market growth just to get back to where they started. And if the percentage loss is higher, that number goes up exponentially. Losing 50% will need a 100% growth.

Now some people may say, "Oh, don't worry about it. You're going to retire. You got another 24 years to make it up." But this is where I insert experience and honesty. The truth is, you will never make that up. Money lost from your portfolio is also money that will not continue to grow for your retirement. You never gain that potential back. I can show people how to recover from losses, and I can explain the sequence of returns, but what is lost is truly gone. This glaring reality should fuel every investment decision.

Relationships Matter

One of the things I learned from my military experience is that relationships matter. When I worked on aviation in the Navy and later ran a commercial aviation business, I met with people, made commitments with people, and followed professional and personal standards in working with people. That's what authentic people did in their work lives and personal lives.

With aviation, it is all about instruction and following the sequence of events. You can't change a tire on an airplane without getting the manual out to make sure that you take the tire off correctly. You must jack it up properly and use a torque wrench to achieve a certain tightness or tension on the lug nut. The standard for lug nut tension is set by years of aircraft research, with proven knowledge that a certain tension will prevent the tire from coming off during flight, takeoff, or landing. Obviously, anyone flying or boarding the plane depends on this critical standard being followed.

Why do I mention proven standards for lug nut tension? Because there's a parallel here. Many people approach finances and financial relationships without following proven advice and professional guidance. They don't want to use a structured platform or do business by the book. Maybe they don't like listening to advice at all – they prefer to learn things on their own. The problem is the wheels on that self-structured financial platform may come off during flight. And when they do, things can quickly escalate to mayday.

I acknowledge that my advice can be hard to follow for some. But I am a firm believer that it's best to tell people what they **need to hear** and not what they *want to hear*. And that's exactly what I do – whether the recipient is going to like me or not.

But here's what my lifetime of experiences has taught me. When I tell people what they need to hear, it puts us both in a position for success. If I do my job, and my client listens and follows my advice, then we will build a successful, ongoing, and long-term relationship. And that's what makes me thrive.

In recognition of how important long-term relationships are to our firm, I will share that we have a client concierge on staff who not only schedules appointments, but also helps all of us reach out to each client to routinely remind them of our commitment to relationships.

And we are adamant about our part of the relationship. Every client, spouse, and their children are in our database. We celebrate birthdays, anniversaries, and set up annual reviews through phone calls, texts, and US mail. We are detail-oriented because that's our part of our commitment. We believe, and want you to know also, that our relationship matters. People put their financial trust in our company, whether I'm working with them or not, and by doing that they deserve the best relationship we can offer.

Insisting on Integrity

When I work with a client, I do my due diligence. I want to know everything that forms their decisions, and I hope to obtain every piece of information that can help me guide them.

I have no doubt clients also find out everything they can about me. I'm happy to help them understand my values, because I want to make sure I'm working with people who have the same integrity as I do. I want to be assured that what people say is what they do.

I also insist on this with the companies and people I network with. I believe that if everybody does what they say they will do, we will all have a win-win relationship.

I have a simple philosophy that I have repeated hundreds of times. I call it the **SWAN mentality for doing business**. SWAN stands for Sleep Well at Night. When I go to bed at night, I want to make sure that whatever I did that day still allows me to sleep; I want to know that I didn't do anything to anybody's detriment.

And frankly, I sleep well.

EUGENE W. HILL, SR.

When people ask what makes D & G Financial Services stand out from the crowd, I tell them that it's the relationships I have built. The primary reason my business has succeeded is because I build relationships. Many of my clients, who now span the United States, have come from referrals and client relationships that I have developed over decades. It is something I take great pride in. I compare business to a good restaurant. If you enjoyed the food, the ambiance was good, and the service was excellent, then you're going to tell your friends about it. That's my daily goal with D & G Financial Services, and I believe we have thus far accomplished it.

Strategy Two: Make Every Day a Saturday

As many people approach retirement, they think every day will be a Saturday. They think they will wake up excited about each day, wondering how much they can pack into their new-found freedom. Which courts will I play today? Which friends will I meet for lunch?

The reality is this thinking can lead to a life lived paycheck-to-paycheck. If there's one thing your working years did, it was keeping you from spending money for the majority of a day. When you work 40 hours a week, you don't have time to meet friends for breakfast, then meet another set for lunch, and hit the mall for some shopping in between. Instead of spending money eight hours a day, you earned it.

It is important to realize most people think their expenditures will go down during retirement, but this is false. In all likelihood, they will go up. This is why planning for retirement is important.

"You Have Your Go-Go Years, Your Slow-Go Years, and Your No-Go Years."

It is often said by financial coach Tom Hegna, **you have your go-go years, your slow-go years, and your no-go years**. This simply means that if you don't plan well and put money aside during your go-go years, you will be faced with slow-go years, and eventually no-go years.

So, if you have invested well during your go-go years, in later life you will be able travel twice a year or take a cruise once a year. If that will cost you $10,000, you will need to budget for it, and this is on top of the funds you will need to maintain your lifestyle. If you don't plan, where is the money going to come from?

Planning will also mean looking at all your assets, including the qualified investments you have made, and managing them properly. The goal is to utilize your savings in the most tax-efficient manner, and to be able to withdraw it tax-free sooner than later. This reason we care about taxes sooner rather than later is because nobody really knows what our tax is going to be next year, or after the next election, or 20 and 30 years from now. The fact is, your money, wherever it is invested, will be withdrawn at some point and Uncle Sam will need to be paid. This may occur because of a RMD (Required Minimum Distribution) at age 73 or because you want to access to your money at an earlier date.

When I meet with people who have not planned well and now owe taxes on their investments, I share this with them: "The government is not taxing to help you out, they're taxing to help themselves out. Because, at the end of the day, we are the government." I say this because we elect the people who represent us, and through them we create the budget that keeps our diverse country safe, our markets open and fair, our personal freedoms secure, and our aspirations and opportunities for success available to everyone.

And I also like to ask people this question: "What's the one thing you can do with money?" It is a simple question, and most of the time I get a straightforward and simple answer.

"I can pay my bills. I can spend it. I can go somewhere." This is what I hear over 90% of the time, and unfortunately, it's what most people think of when they hear the word money – something they can buy.

That's when I introduce the **Principle of 70/30.**

Strategy Three: The Principle of 70/30

The 70/30 principle is something I came up with and have implemented at D & G Financial. It is drawn from my Christian background and my church involvement. We use it in our individual planning platforms, we teach it in our organizational workshops, we use it when we analyze a portfolio, and we speak about it in our stewardship training at our church.

We also use a catchy phrase that has been trademarked. It is a theme I use in my meetings, workshops, and coaching sessions as a guide for each person's decision making. It goes like this: ***Money - Reverse the curse, give, save, invest, and live off the rest.*** I build upon this phrase by educating each client and making sure they understand how money should be used and applied. I also say this to anyone I speak with, whether it be a phone call, in a personal relationship, or at a professional meeting.

This then becomes the basis for my **Principle of 70/30**. This means you use 70% of your net income to support your lifestyle, and 30% to give, save, and invest. And when I use 30%, I'm recommending 10% go to your church or a non-profit of your choice, 10% be set aside as a savings for unforeseen events, and 10% be put into a long-term investment for your retirement.

The First 10%

Many people forget (or refuse to believe) that everything belongs to God, and we are to be good stewards of the gifts we have been given. If we do that, we honor what He says. And I make no apologies for using this expression because I truly believe that God will never give you anything and add sorrow to it.

I believe you can't get a Christian worldview for your money if you're not talking to someone with a Christian worldview. The word of God says in Malachi 3: 6: "For I am the Lord, I change not." And later, in verse 10, he says: "If you bring your tithe and offering to the storehouse there will be meat to eat." Then he offers a test: "And try Me now in this, if I will not open for you the windows of heaven and pour out for you such blessing that there will not be room enough to receive it."

I truly believe that His words are true, and I follow this philosophy by taking 10% off my gross income and giving that to my church or another charity. I do this because I believe my money is going to a place that follows the same core values that I believe in. And if this charity or church has a 501(c)(3), then I can write that off from my taxes. That is true stewardship and a personally satisfying way to give.

It's also worth pointing out that when people pay taxes, which can be much higher than 10%, the government can use that money in whatever way they want. And many times, those taxes may support expenditures that those same people may not champion.

"When You are a Good Steward of Your Money and Understand What God Has Done for Us, The First Thing on Your Mind Should Be to Give Your Offerings to the Storehouse."

Additionally, I subscribe to the philosophy that **when you are a good steward of your money and understand what God has done for us, then the first thing on your mind should be to give your offerings to the storehouse.** This is the Christian perspective I follow of giving a tithe or 10% to your church, or to a non-profit organization that supports your belief system.

To me, this 10% is a critical first step in understanding the discipline and commitments needed when working with money.

The Second 10%

The second financial commitment I recommend is creating a savings plan. Some might say this is putting money aside for a rainy day, but I prefer to think of it as building a solid foundation for your financial future. From my experience, many of the people I speak with have not done this. Statistics I have read indicate that 70% of people who are 65 and older have less than $25,000 saved, and 40% of all American households have set aside less than $15,000.

These figures don't indicate if they are gainfully employed, fully retired, or their lifestyle. But one thing is certain: every person involved in these statistics is getting older and moving towards retirement. And each one of them will experience a sudden need for money.

The key to this second 10% is putting something aside for an emergency, such as a death in the family, or a broken water heater, or an unexpected car repair. If you don't plan for those events, how will you pay for them? I believe this savings percentage is the answer.

"I Want My Clients to Understand How Savings Work, How It Can Improve Their Credit, and How It Can Help Them Understand the Importance of Financial Discipline."

If a person utilizes this in their planning, they can overcome sudden jumps in inflation, interest rate increases, the dot-com bubble from 1999-2000, and the market fluctuations of 1989 and 2008. I want my clients to understand how savings work, the impact it has on their credit, and how it can help them understand the importance of financial discipline.

The Third 10%

The third part of the 70/30 Rule is a commitment to take a portion of your income and invest it for your retirement. This would include Individual Retirement Accounts (IRAs) such as 401(k)s, 403(b)s, or other independent investments. This is investing for yourself and your financial future when your career has ended.

This 10% also includes investing in your children. It could be for their college education, their wedding, or maybe their honeymoon. And if for some reason they don't attend a trade school or college and they never marry, it still could be used to give them a head start in their adult life.

When clients have chosen this commitment, I recommend they be coachable and willing to learn. Investments always come with a degree of risk, so I ask them to become well-educated and aware of the tax advantages that come with an investment portfolio.

Today's companies no longer offer defined benefit programs or pensions. Instead, they encourage you to invest in tax-deferred qualified plans. Today's tax environment is excellent with some of the lowest federal taxes in years. I'm not a prognosticator who can tell you what taxes will be in 5 or 10 years, but knowing our country's inflationary cycles, our increasing debt, and the growth of our social programs, I'm putting my money on the likelihood that taxes will rise.

Most companies will set up or provide information for these qualified investments, which were established when the Revenue Act of 1978 was passed. I have also set these up for many of my clients so they can do an in-service rollout of their 401k into an IRA or whatever the platform may be.

Some of my younger clients, in their thirties or forties, have begun these plans. They work for a company that offers a 3% match to their 3% contribution. That's great. But what I encourage them to do, and what we set up for them, is a plan where they match their company's 3% with a 7% contribution. This way they can commit to a full 10% investment. We do this using an insurance component, a Roth IRA, or a non-qualified annuity, or whatever the case may be.

Whatever platform we use, our objective is to invest after-tax money now while taxes are at an all-time low, and then distribute them tax-free later. There is no guarantee that taxes will continue to be this low five, ten, or twenty years from now. And most experts expect it to rise. For these reasons, the perfect time to put your after-tax money into an investment account and make it tax-free forever is now.

And if your company is not doing a qualitied match, we can set up a platform that provides liquidity so that you can access your money, pay it back, use it again, and yet have no tax consequences. These are the conversations we have with a lot of people, and we also try to make sure they fully understand the commitment and benefits that are involved.

The Remaining 70%
The remaining 70% represents your household budget and includes everything from your mortgage, your utilities, the clothes you wear, the vacation you take, the gifts you give, and the food on your table. Some of these expenses are fixed, but others can vary widely because of inflation, or unforeseen expenses, such as the pandemic. If you can manage this at 70%, you will be on your way to a worry-free lifestyle.

I say this because I have met people who live a lifestyle they can't afford, and many times they do this only to impress other people. They worry more about what others think than they worry about staying within their budget. There's an old phrase I often use that goes like this: People spend money they don't have to buy stuff they can't afford to impress people they don't even like. I've seen this over and over. I hope my guidance in this book keeps you from following this same path.

EUGENE W. HILL, SR.

"People Spend Money They Don't Have to Buy Stuff They Can't Afford to Impress People They Don't Even Like."

In a perfect world, I hope to emphasize the importance of staying within your budget constraints and spending less than you make. When you do this, you will secure your financial future and the future of your family's financial security.

Some people buy mega mansions, and there's nothing wrong with that if you can comfortably afford it. But many people work multiple jobs and feel frustrated and miserable, just to have more house than they can use. If I purchase a home with seven bedrooms and only need two or three – and I am always worried about my money – would I ever enjoy living there? That extra square footage offers nothing but stress.

I am blessed to have a business office and a home office, and my home also has a kitchen, a family room, a master bedroom, and of course a bathroom. But that is just part of my house. The rest I don't even use. So, if you have budget constraints, why do you buy more than you need? For many of the people I speak to, it's to impress others.

I truly believe you will not have an impact on your future or your family's future if you are more concerned about what others think than your own wellbeing. This single issue can defeat people, and those who are around them. It is really a living lie that can prevent people from reaching financial freedom.

Most wealthy people – and by wealthy, I mean millionaires and billionaires – drive cars that are four or five years old and are fully paid for. Instead of making a monthly car payment of $500, they use that money to reinvest in their business or future security. They don't waste it on something that is not important to their lifestyle.

My strategy, and the strategy of most financially successful people, is to look at money from a holistic viewpoint. I mentioned this earlier in the book. Every penny should be just as important as every $100. The interest rate and fees you would have spent to take on a car loan can be better used on life insurance. Also, the $30,000 price tag may suddenly drop to $27,500 if you are able to pay with cash. That's the power money can have when you approach your budget from a holistic vantage point.

When I mention the 70/30 Rule to my clients, I liken it to football. I played football when I was younger and my son played football in college and also coached college football. The analogy here is that in football, you have a position you play, and with this you stay in your lane. You have a role to play in making the team successful, whether it be blocking or running or kicking.

So, if you truly want to win the game, you stick to the rules and follow each of the percentages. It is almost like building a specialty team for each of these four principles – a team that is trained to succeed in their lane.

I say this because I have seen people spend $200 or more/month at the mall or making purchases and through other venues. They would do this month after month for years. That's $2,400 a year and $4,800 in just two years. That's almost $5,000 that I believe could have been invested in their future.

"I've Seen People Buy Things They Don't Need, Then Stockpile Them."

I've also seen people buy things they don't need and then stockpile them. They buy clothing and shoes, golf clubs that pile up in their homes. And when they have too much stuff, they rent a storage unit and fill it with items they will never bring back to their house. What's the logic of this?

Every successful company plans for a "just in time" inventory so they don't have to store the items they didn't sell. They constantly move their products out the door. This is an efficient business model, and something the average person should follow. I tell people to buy only what they need, use it until it wears out or is no longer important to their lifestyle, then sell it or dispose of it. This also happens to be the most efficient way to manage your budget.

I have also found that much of this spending is done without any budget constraint and is a mindset that many people follow blindly. This typically continues until they establish a different relationship with their money and decide to manage it, save it, invest it, and make it work for them. In today's economy, you can't expect to sit back and watch it come in, unless you purposefully protect it and shield it.

Developing A Spending Plan

A lot of people I have met don't have a spending plan, or more colloquially, a budget. They make a thousand dollars a week and they spend a thousand dollars a week. They do this week after week after week and wonder where all their money went. They don't manage it or track it or understand where it has gone.

So, what I like to do is have them create a systematic way to account for each expenditure for just 3 or 4 months. When they do this, and categorize each item, then I can begin a process of identifying where they can save their money and where they can refocus their costs.

Recently, inflation has complicated this issue. It's hard to set up a spending plan when the prices for products are soaring. Groceries have gone up, real estate values have grown, mortgages are now 6% or 7%, and interest rates are much higher. If you are retired and on a fixed income, you will need to do a better job of itemizing and re-evaluate your basic needs. Many people were not prepared for this kind of inflation late in life.

RETIREMENT MONEY GUIDE

Strategy Four: Maximizing Medicare and Social Security

Medicare

We have a Medicare component we use in our practice. We introduce clients to this when they are transitioning from work to retirement. But as I said earlier, I like to call this re-fire not re-tire. Today, with the Affordable Care Act now 13 years old, the federal government is more interested in preventive care than they have ever been.

They want to keep you healthy, because in the long run your illness and disabilities will cost the government more through their other social programs. This is when our firm can step in to supplement Medicare with long-term care insurance riders. We use all sorts of platforms to structure your medical and retirement care depending on your need. This wasn't always the case, but I think we are there now: ***you will most likely need life insurance sooner or later.***

Insurance companies really operate as actuaries. That's how they stay in business. They look at various factors, like your health, your bad habits, and your genetic factors, and they build out a pricing structure that makes it likely they will make money in the end.

For their health insurance policies, insurers are not going to take on a risk that already exists. So, if you come in with a medical condition or illness that is already visible or documented, you will need to find a way to self-insure. But rest assured, we can help you self-insure, as well.

Government entities at the federal, state, and local level have always required people to carry an insurance policy if they are driving a car, using a mortgage to buy a house, or opening a business that serves the public. These policies have been in place to protect you and your properties from damage, and also protect you from lawsuits that may arise because of your ownership. In a way, they have come about because people want protection against financial loss.

But the government has never mandated health insurance, except for a small percentage of people who are covered under the Affordable Care Act. So, in essence, you are asked to insure your car, your house, your business, and just about everything you own, but not your own health. That's strange, isn't it?

Let me be clear: **I am <u>not</u> advocating that the government needs to step in and force you to buy health insurance**. On the contrary, I am suggesting that the government wants *you* to step up to the plate and take care of yourself.

While we are on the subject of Medicare, which can also include Medicaid and other health policies, I want to speak briefly about ADLs (Activities of Daily Life). These include all activities that are related to personal care, such as showering, dressing, getting in and out of bed or a chair, walking, using the toilet, and eating. Whether or not you can do all these functions without help will be a key to your eligibility for long term care insurance.

A lot of people tend to think that our government or social security or Medicare will pay for long-term care, but this is not true. What I have found is that aging is one of those subjects that people don't really want to think about until they are getting slapped in the face by it. They don't want to learn all of the pieces that are involved until they are faced with their own retirement or disability. As a financial advisor, I am obligated to cover this subject and update them about their options. And frankly, this is one of those "I'm going to tell you the truth because it's best for you" topics.

Some of the people I meet with, because of their economic status, have qualified for Medicaid. But to do this, they will need to document all of their assets including their savings account and the value of their home. Some consideration is given for the spouse of that individual, but if they need to go to a nursing home, they will need to turn all of their resources over. And these actions are not reversible. Whether you live in a nursing home only a week or for years, the assets you turn over will *not* come back to the family. This is just one of the reasons I am not in favor of moving retirement portfolios to assisted care facilities.

In contrast to this scenario, I believe your best option is to have a strategy in place that will provide for you on your own terms. This would include the funding of home healthcare or redirecting money to a family member who could help. This is not a cookie-cutter approach; this is complicated and requires a lot of pre-planning. To make this happen I use several formulas and calculations. There are a lot of additional strategies I bring to the plate, but everything is a result of asking the right questions and helping people put a plan together.

Social Security

The Social Security Act was signed into law in 1935. Since then, for better or worse, it has become the major source of retirement income for most Americans. The average Social Security benefit in November 2022 was $1,551 and the total cost of the Social Security program for the year 2021 was $1.145 trillion, or about 5 percent of our nation's GDP. This is not only a big deal for America, but also a big deal for most of my clients.

"To Most People, Social Security Does Not Seem Important Until They Start Looking at Their Retirement."

To most people, Social Security does not seem important until they start looking at their retirement. This usually happens in their late 50s or early 60s, as they begin to worry about their future income stream.

Social Security is really something you purchase over a number of years. Some people I have met have put money into it for over 40 years. By buying into it for that long a time, each person would be wise to gain back the maximum value of their purchase. Obviously, no one would want to buy something and not receive the greatest return on their investment. This is where I can help.

For almost anyone who has paid into Social Security, the decision on when to withdraw can affect the amount on your monthly checks, and potentially the total amount you will receive. In addition to your age, the factors that influence this decision the most are how much you have contributed, your current health and potential for health issues, and the other sources of retirement revenue you will use, like your investments and qualified accounts.

Because retirement is not one-size-fits-all, decisions on when to begin your Social Security checks will vary widely. What I want to do here is to list some of the age factors that are most important.

- The youngest age you can start taking Social Security is 62. At this age you will receive 75% of the full retirement benefit you could have received.
- With each subsequent month this percentage goes higher, for example:
- At 63 the percentage has risen to 80%
- At 64 the percentage has risen to 86.7%
- At 65 it is 93.3%
- At 66 it is 100%
- At 67 it is 108%
- And at 70 you will reach your highest potential of 132%

Obviously, waiting until you are 66 or even 70 to draw from Social Security will benefit your monthly income the most, and if you live 25 more years into your 90s, your net sum will also be much higher. However, if you work (and therefore keep adding to Social Security) until you are 67 or older, the percentages don't change, but your monthly checks may go higher because you are continuing to pay into the system. Another recent plus is that Social Security checks just matched recent inflation numbers with an 8.7% raise.

However, aside from theoretical return on investment, I always want clients to be realistic about their health. If your health is poor, if you have been seriously injured in an accident, if your parents or siblings have experienced health issues, or if you are genetically predisposed in some way to a shortened lifespan, then you will want to consider taking Social Security at 62. This will gain you the best return on your investment.

One of the best aspects of beginning at age 62 is you can continue to work and contribute, you can still apply for benefits, you can do both, or you can do neither. But again, the key here is your health, and whether you have other financial investments you can draw on for income during your retirement.

When I meet with someone, I look at all these factors and try to figure out what makes the most sense for their circumstances and age. As I've said before, I believe that every person deserves an individualized approach to their retirement, and with that a full analysis of their Social Security benefits.

I also want to share that when my wife retired, she decided not to draw her social security. She waited until she could maximize it. Now, between her pension and social security, she has a decent income that she will never outlive. I know that if something happens to me, she's going to be comfortable. That's proper planning and using the system to your advantage. That's what I wish for my clients, as well.

RETIREMENT MONEY GUIDE

Strategy Five: The Secure Act 2.0 and Legacy Planning

Secure Act 2.0

The Secure Act 2.0 was signed into law on December 29, 2022. With its passage came more than 90 new retirement plan provisions. These include new tax savings, mandated auto-enrollment plans, and additional flexibility for investors.

As in the past, the IRS allows penalty-free withdrawals from IRAs or other tax qualified accounts beginning at age 59½, with a 10% penalty imposed on distributions prior to that. But this updated law raised the age for when Required Minimum Distributions (RMDs) must be taken. What was age 72 is now 73. Moreover, your RMD dollar amount increases over the years.

Although this allows people to extend the life of their qualified accounts, it will likely give them fewer years to enjoy the fruits of their investment. But, of course, this has always been the tradeoff for qualified accounts.

With the Secure Act, the government is looking at spousal beneficiaries of these accounts. When these qualified accounts are inherited, they will be taxed. The government is developing strategies to make sure they have access and control of your money. But at D & G Financial, our platforms are designed to keep you in control.

> *"If You Develop a Plan While You are Still Alive and Working, YOU Will Control the and Taxation of Your Money."*

I can't emphasize this enough: if you develop a plan while you are still alive and working, **you** get to control the disbursement and taxation of your money. If you don't do anything and you die, you hand that control over to the government, where they will decide the taxes your beneficiaries will pay. When given that choice, I don't know too many people who say, "Oh, I trust the government to do what I wanted."

Many of the people I work with have a disconnect about this issue. They've been working for 20 years and have set up an account where taxes are deferred and then paid when the money is distributed. They were never told about Roth accounts or paid taxes on this income when it was earned.

However, with today's near-record-low-income tax rates, it has become increasingly attractive to cash out these deferred-tax accounts and pay the taxes up front. In nearly all cases, that is our guidance. Paying the taxes now and convert your investments to another tax-free vehicle, so that when you withdraw your principle later, it will be tax free. You've already paid your share.

And don't get me wrong. I believe everyone should pay their fair share to the government. But I also don't believe you need to be foolish about it. Use tax strategies and make sure you understand how the system works. If you don't understand the difference between marginal tax rates and excessive tax rates, allow us to help you. Most people don't realize the significant impact good guidance can have on the amount you ultimately pay in taxes. Indeed, if you use the proper tools and do the proper planning, your tax rate can be as low as 5%.

There are essentially two ways to do this, and I describe these in detail when I work with clients. One way is through various forms of life insurance and the other is through Roth IRAs. And in the event a person is not insurable, and they haven't set up a Roth IRA, then we can do a Roth conversion to put them in the same standing. There is a solution for everyone.

Legacy Planning and Long-Term Care
When we talk to people about retirement planning, we also cover their legacy planning. Legacy planning is retirement planning in a tax-efficient manner so that your estate can grow tax-deferred and tax-free.

If you understand how the system works, and how the Internal Revenue Code and tax laws can benefit you, you can use them to your advantage. This is especially important in legacy planning. When I meet with clients or when I'm doing annual reviews, I always put this on the agenda for discussion. And it's not something most people think about because it can be somewhat intangible.

Our legacy planning platforms allow people in various states to do revocable life insurance trusts. Every component needed for proper planning is in these platforms. If the situation changes because of divorce or death, we can easily make changes on our computers. We combine a personal touch and understanding with the technology we have built to make sure people understand the value and direction of their financial legacy.

Another point I make comes in the form of a question I ask my senior clients: "Tell me; if you leave money to your grandkids, are they going to receive it over a 10-year spread, or all at once?" I tell them that if this is not done properly, if your estate is restructured for tax efficiency, Uncle Sam is going to wind up with 30, 40, or even 50% of your money. This is money you have earned and earmarked for your legacy, *and you've already paid taxes on once*, that you hope provides generational wealth for your family. Why would anyone want to hand Uncle Sam another 50%? Only those who are unprepared do so.

Generally speaking, the IRS does not want you to distribute your estate to your spouse or anyone else without it being taxed. But with proper planning, and using our planning platforms, your legacy can be secured and your taxes minimalized.

I call myself a safe-money guy. I want to know where my money is spent during my lifetime and where it will go after I pass away. I want to earmark everything in my beneficiary statement, whether it be for a charity or not, because I truly believe that what I give away, what I create as my legacy, is a reflection of my belief in the Dominion and Glory of God.

"We Call Our Seniors Golden Millennial Achievers."

At my church, where I serve as associate pastor, we call our seniors Golden Millennial Achievers. Unfortunately, a lot of these people have insurance policies they purchased years ago that may not be as adequate now that they are older. What we do is re-evaluate their current policies to make sure they are adequate, and many times add other policies that may address long-term care or the potential for critical illness.

These additional policies can help children and other family members make financially sound decisions for you if ever needed. And these policies can provide in-home care to help you avoid nursing homes that sometimes charge exorbitant fees and ask you to redirect your estate. No matter what, we find that reviewing insurance policies and retirement plans brings peace and comfort for everyone. And I thoroughly enjoy doing that.

Strategy Six: The Younger Generation

While most retirement guidance tends to skip the younger generations, I'm not one to do so. In recent years, I've noticed that many couples are waiting until they are older to marry and will therefore bring separate investment accounts into the marriage. Some will keep their earnings in separate accounts, and many want to protect their own earnings in case their marriage or partnership is dissolved. These changing social dynamics complicate financial planning, tax savings, and inheritance. So, in reality, I find the younger generations are in need of good financial planning even more than their parents were at their age.

When I encounter situations like these, I make no excuses about my biblical viewpoint. I don't believe you can follow a Christian worldview in financial planning unless you are someone with a Christian worldview. So, if there is a family unit, whether they are partners or husband and wife, it is not her money or his money. It is their money. That's my belief.

I also believe that some people get caught up separating their accounts because of cultural pressures or an independent mindset. They are worried that if something happens, they want to hold onto their little nest egg. But I believe that all two-person relationships are 50/50, and together their relationship is 100%. No matter how much each person contributes, it should be a win-win relationship.

> ***"I Believe That All Two-Person Relationships Are 50/50, and Together, Their Relationship is 100%."***

Sometimes I hear people say, "Okay, you've got this," or "This is mine." But what I encourage them to do is sit down and spend time together with me. I want them to look at all their expenditures and write them down so that both of them can put all of their financial pieces together. Many times, couples don't reveal to each other all of their financial goals. This can work to their detriment and is a paradigm we need to change.

In my practice, my team knows that if it's a husband and wife, we will want to work with both of them. To create a successful plan, we really need to have both ~~of them~~ meet in our offices or on a Zoom call. Because if I talk to the man or the woman and their partner is missing, I will need to share that same information again, and I will need to confront the rejections and opinions all over again. This is certainly not an efficient way of addressing both of their interests.

College Funding Plans

When we talk to clients about investing, we also discuss college planning. This is something I bring up when I first meet with clients who have younger children. I tell them that it is a much better approach to invest in their child's future, and to have gains on that investment, than it is to be straddled with high-interest student loans years later. College funding also comes with tax advantages.

These investment strategies are commonly called a 529 Plans. They were initially created by states such as Michigan, Ohio, and Florida in the 1980s but were eventually incorporated into the federal tax code under Section 529. Although these plans are still state sponsored, you can use a plan from any state. They have now become the primary way for families to invest in their child's post-secondary education.

The advantages of a 529 plan include:

- Federal income tax benefits, and sometimes state tax benefits.
- Low maintenance fees of $10 to $25 per year per account.
- High contribution limits – with investment limits of over $100,000 in several states.
- Flexibility to change the beneficiary or roll over some of the money.
- Favorable financial aid treatment from many colleges.

I encourage parents to choose a college plan for their child as early as possible, hopefully soon after they're born. This is a discipline they need to make to avoid higher education expenses later. These plans are used across the board by average income Americans, as well as the wealthy. This early-on discipline is an important trade-off for the costs that will be incurred later.

"I Encourage Parents to Choose a College Plan for Their Child as Early as Possible, Hopefully Soon after They are Born."

Any investment in the market will need cautious management, but 529s have a lot of flexibility. They are controlled by the account owner – the parents in this case – and the beneficiaries can always be changed. So, if scholarship money becomes available for a child, then other children or grandchildren can be designated. And if this investment is not used to fund education, as much as $35,000 per beneficiary can be rolled back into the owner's qualified account to augment their retirement.

I used to tell clients that "If you have a platform earmarked for college, that money would have to be used for college. And if you took distributions from it, it would now be taxable." But under the new Secure Act 2.0 guidelines, if you have a 529 investment, it is possible to roll over some of it into a Roth IRA. You will still have restrictions on when you can access it, but at least they're not counting it toward your deferred platforms for years to come.

A 529 plan also allows a participant to set up a tax-advantaged account that allows a beneficiary to use the funds for qualified education expenses. The participant deposits after-tax money in the account, and it can grow tax-deferred and then be tapped tax-free for relevant expenses.

What I tell my younger clients now is to put college funding strategies in place early so that they are tax-free versus taxable, and make them available regardless of the family dynamics that may arise. Because the alternative is what most end up doing: what I call late-stage college planning. It's the "Oops, we haven't made plans yet" plan, and it doesn't come with nearly any of the benefits of proper planning.

In the end, I believe that each individual and each family unit is unique, and I am just the facilitator of their agenda and what they want to accomplish. And that's an honor.

Student Loans

Another important issue with college funding is student loans. I have met people who have graduated from college with debt that they will never be able to repay. They have a degree, but that degree will never pay them back what they have spent on college. In this case, I encourage parents to help by doing some due diligence, so their child is not caught up by predator loans and are stuck with monthly payments that go on seemingly forever.

I also have clients who have borrowed money to put their child through college, only to have them drop out and never get a degree. Because they signed for the loan, they are obligated to pay it off. These situations cannot be resolved easily, but can be avoided by better financial planning. I have a platform for this that can help them address this issue.

"College Funding is Something That is Very Dear to My Hear."

College funding is something that is very dear to my heart because I'm adamant that children should get an opportunity to have a higher education. And if scholarships are offered, this money can be used to fund a graduate degree or a down payment on a home. I see this as part of the legacy a parent can give their child.

Wedding Plans

When I speak with clients who have daughters, I tell them: "You have three things you need to address. One, you need to plan for your retirement, two, you need to set aside money for their college education, and three, you will also need to save for their wedding day. For some families, this is a big deal and can be very expensive. I know some families intend to compromise on this issue, but with today's cultural standards in America, most parents of daughters will end up paying for the wedding.

In a perfect world, parents start putting together plans for their children's educations and weddings when the children are young. Then, by the time the kids turn 18 and are ready for college, it's not a matter of whether they choose a college, it's where they will go to college. That's exactly what we did for our three boys.

I also consider this type of investing a no-regrets scenario. No matter the path your child takes, you will be able to provide. If your child chooses to marry, you have set aside money to cover it. If not, you have a nest egg for them that can jump start their career. To most parents, the marriage and career choices of their children are very important, and if they are something you champion, then can support their choices in unparalleled ways.

The Next Steps

The Key to Prosperity Is Cash Flow

I tell people that the key to prosperity is cash flow. It's not assets, it's cash flow. This is because all the homes or businesses you own are assets on your accounting ledger, but they are only assets if they can take care of themselves. For example, if I have an investment property that is rented out, and the mortgage payment is $1,000 per month, and I'm bringing in $1,500 in monthly rental, then that's truly an asset, because it's debt-servicing itself.

But if I'm sitting in a house and paying a $1,000 per month, and I still owe $100,000 or $200,000 on it and have no equity to speak of, then that is not really an asset. It may seem like an asset because it is the home you have purchased, but for accounting purposes, it is not.

Recently, some areas of our country have seen property values rise substantially. Many of my clients have gained $100,000 or more in equity in just the past two years. But this gain in assets is only available when your home is sold.

Coaches, Agents, and Advisors

I frequently ask people what their favorite athletes and teams are. Do they have a favorite college basketball team, or professional baseball team? Who do they think will win the Super Bowl? And who are their favorite actors or movies, or television shows?

When they answer, I mention that every one of those individuals or teams has an agent, coach, coordinator, advisor, or director available to help them succeed. ***In today's complicated world, no one can make it to the top without help.***

"In Today's Complicated World, No One Makes it To the Top without Help."

This is also true when you want to succeed financially. The wealthy will have several advisors available to help them and I believe the average American needs at least one. Managing your money is not a DIY project, because all the components, such as taxes, fees, interest rates, deductions, rollovers, and investment risks, require someone who has the skills and resources to coordinate the components for your benefit.

I tell people that when it comes to money, you need someone who will hold you accountable, someone who will tell you what you need to hear, and someone who can help you overcome the losses and build for your future. Sometimes this may not be what you want to hear, but if you are working with an advisor with years of experience and a track record of success, I guarantee you will benefit. Just like Hollywood stars and pro athletes, you will have a much better chance of being the best.

But there's one caveat: to be successful you must also be coachable. I have heard it said that if you keep doing what you are doing, you're going to get what you always got. So, if your financial situation has not been successful, you need a successful financial coach. And you need to *be* coachable.

You've heard it said that there is no free lunch. This is certainly true when it comes to managing your finances. If you want to put away money each month and be worth a million dollars in 10 years, you will need advice. If you want to change your financial dynamics, you will need advice. If your taxes are complicated, you will need advice. And if you want the best return on your investments, you will need advice.

Sometimes people make decisions based on what it will cost them, but when it comes to experienced and trusted financial advice, I believe it is well worth the investment.

Teachers and Nurses

I see a lot of teachers and nurses, and because of this I am very attuned to their needs. As I said earlier, my wife is a registered nurse and recently retired. Because most nurses and teachers have worked for non-profit organizations, they have 403(b) investment accounts. This is especially true with public school teachers. Unfortunately, many of these individuals have never sought out retirement advice and have just assumed the disbursements from their qualified account plus their Social Security checks will be sufficient to maintain their lifestyle.

But in many cases, just six months after they retire, they are back working again. This is not because they want to work or have a passion for what they are doing. Instead, it's because **they didn't plan well and need the money.** For these people, who have been dedicated professionals all their life, good financial planning is essential.

What I do with many of these individuals is roll their money over to a traditional IRA. In fact, if you have a Roth 403(b) you must roll it over into a Roth IRA. Another important consideration for teachers and nurses who want to retire early is the 10% penalty the IRS will charge you if you withdraw from your qualified account before you reach 59½ years old.

As I said earlier, the more you can contribute to Social Security and your qualified account, and the longer you wait to withdraw from them, the better your retirement income will be.

Money Pays for It, But Good Health Buys It

We have talked about family legacies and good financial planning, but when you get down to the facts, money may pay for it, but good health buys it. This is especially true when dealing with life insurance, where the longer you wait to purchase it, the more it will cost. Additionally, if you have known health issues, the cost may be more than you can afford.

As I mentioned earlier, insurance companies are actuaries, and they are in the business of making a profit. But I don't work for any insurance companies; I work for my client. By being an independent advisor, and wanting to offer the best advice out there, I'm going to find you the best company for your unique situation.

Concluding Thoughts

If your car needs service, you go to an auto technician. If your body needs a procedure, you go to a doctor or specialist. More than ever, the same logic applies to financial health. The laws are updated constantly, and new investment and insurance options are added daily. Unless your full-time job is to follow these changes, you will find it nearly impossible to guide yourself.

I know far too many people who have either lost significant resources or missed out on the best path forward simply because they didn't stop to consult a financial advisor. If not for you, I encourage you to do it for your legacy and future generations. And I hope I have the pleasure of meeting you in the process.

Made in the USA
Middletown, DE
10 March 2024